Your Living Legacy

An Important Conversation

Christopher Cousins, ChFC®, RICP®

<u>Other books in The Family Legacy Center's series:</u>

Women and Legacy: *It's More Than You Might Think*

familylegacycenter.com

To my wife Susie and my daughters Ella and Olivia. My love for you is timeless and your support means everything.

Acknowledgements

Without the encouragement and confidence of a number of important people, I wouldn't have completed this book.

To my parents—your support, guidance, wisdom, and patience made me who I am today.

To Ken Grace, Pat Marody, Turner Thompson, and my entire Financial Architects family—your collective commitment to making a difference in our industry and in people's lives inspires me every day. Thank you for the opportunity to join your team.

Finally, thank you to my friend Joanne Giardini-Russell. I appreciate your passion, inspiration, and motivation—all of which were instrumental in helping me accomplish this project. You are impressively consistent in your efforts to advocate for the importance of legacy planning.

Contents

Foreword by Fanchon Stinger 1

Introduction.. 4

1: Defining Legacy 6

2: An Important Conversation.......................16

3: Common Legacy Misconceptions.............24

4: Living Legacy 36

5: Practical Applications of Legacy..............44

6: Continuing the Conversation 56

Epilogue.. 59

About the Author.. i

Forward

Everyone will leave a legacy. We can't escape it: whether it is intentional or unintentional, you *will* leave a legacy. What will it be? What are you doing today to contribute to the development of your legacy? Do you even know how to begin answering that question? And if you can't answer it, how will you ever build true wealth? Perhaps building wealth is less connected to how much money you accumulate, than to the living legacy you create on your journey toward expanding your wealth beyond material gain. If so, where and how do we begin?

In this book, Chris Cousins takes you on a journey that masterfully challenges and corrects the commonly understood concept of legacy. If you want to create a lasting legacy for several generations of your family, you can! If you want to align your legacy with your God-given responsibility to do so, it is possible. Chris breaks down every part of the legacy equation: values, experience, passions, and resources. Once you identify how to calculate what you want your legacy to be—then, and only then, will you be able to chart a path toward affecting multiple generations of your family.

As part of Financial Architects, Inc. in Farmington Hills, Michigan, Chris has changed the way I view the responsibilities that come with building, sustaining, and putting wealth to work for my children and their children's children. I've come to understand that legacy planning begins by identifying your core values and shifting from a micro world view to a macro world view. The foundation of wealth planning is identifying what you want your legacy to be, taking action to shape that legacy, and seeing it begin to play out *before* you die.

In the following chapters, Chris beautifully illustrates how knowing your legacy has more to do with how you live your life than what happens after your death. Achieving sustainable wealth and implementing a multigenerational legacy begins with a critical paradigm shift and by reading this book, you're taking the first step toward that shift. Chris reminds us that we need to "think less about what happens after your death and more about your choices while you're alive and well."

Chris provides a road map that will change generations of families and wealth. He shows how being intentional about our priorities, being aware of how our values influence our interactions, and remaining thoughtful about how we manage and spend our money allow us each to have a very active role in shaping our legacy.

Legacy isn't about how you're remembered in death, but how your life is lived every day and how you affect the people around you. Chris gives you the formula for achieving sustainable, generational wealth, not by just amassing more dollars, but by using those dollars to create a living legacy.

Thus this book is appropriately titled *Your Living Legacy: An Important Conversation*. After reading it, though, I'd say it's not just an important conversation—it's the *most important* conversation.

So let's start talking.

Fanchon Stinger

Evening News Anchor, Fox59, Indianapolis

August 4, 2014

Introduction

Your Living Legacy: *An Important Conversation*

During my twenty years in financial services, I've spent time with many different types of people in various financial circumstances. As my colleagues and I have worked to foster legacy conversations with our clients and industry associates, I've noticed that the most common notion people have about legacy is that most people who leave a legacy do so because they have a great deal of wealth. Furthermore, it is assumed that many others don't leave a legacy because they don't or can't provide an inheritance to their heirs. My colleagues and I fundamentally reject this notion. While money often plays a big role in how legacies play out, the greater conversation around the idea of a legacy needs to be further clarified and expanded beyond exclusively financial concerns. This is among the first in a number of publications from The Family Legacy Center that will fully explore the many facets of legacy. My goals for this book are to briefly discuss legacy and the important concepts surrounding it from a number of perspectives, to explore common misconceptions about legacy, and to argue that our legacies are created actively and daily.

You can leverage your core values and experiences with your passion and resources to enhance your legacy as a whole person. The end result is that regardless of wealth level, legacy starts with each individual. It is up to each of us to create something powerful to leave behind.

In 2013, I started The Family Legacy Center with my associate and cofounder, Joanne Giardini-Russell. Our objective was to support the important work we do at Financial Architects, Inc., by developing and advocating for a more nuanced and expansive understanding of legacy.

We began with a series of client and non-client interviews that offered new insights into people's preconceived ideas about legacy and their goals. Our journey of discovery has been enlightening and we look forward to further exploration into this multifaceted and fascinating topic. We believe that through the development of structured conversations and tools, each of us—regardless of net worth—can be thoughtful and deliberate in planning and implementing his or her legacy.

Christopher Cousins, ChFC®, RICP®

Financial Architects, Inc.

39395 W. Twelve Mile Rd. Suite 102
Farmington Hills, MI 48331
chris@financialarch.com

(financialarch.com)
(familylegacycenter.com)

1

Defining Legacy

Legacy. What does the word mean? Does it mean that something of value is left to relatives or charities after we are gone? Does it refer primarily to money and possessions? Is a legacy more substantial because someone bequeathed a valuable donation? Or could it have more to do with how someone is remembered after this life, the footprint he or she leaves on the life of another? Maybe legacy is less connected to money than we assume.

The reality is that legacy has as many different meanings as there are different types of people. We will all leave a legacy, good or bad. It's not optional. We'll all leave something— trivial or meaningful—behind at the end of our lives that will define us. You can choose whether your legacy will be an unplanned and unintentional byproduct or the result of a series of proactive choices.

For example, we likely all know people so frugal that their legacies will be that they were cheap. What about people so focused on achieving success that they leave legacies of shallow, unfulfilling relationships? Then there are people who are all about having fun, but aren't serious about much; their legacies could be a string of unreached potential.

What about those people everyone loves to be around, but who can't be counted on to come through when they're needed most? What about the brilliant people with amazing potential who live unhealthy lifestyles that contribute to a shortened life? Or successful entrepreneurs who leave the people around them feeling unappreciated and exploited. What are their legacies? All of these cases illustrate how your actions and choices play significant roles in how your legacy builds over time.

During our more than twenty years of experience in the wealth management business, my colleagues and I have noticed observable patterns in how personal legacies develop and play out.

Legacy is understood differently based on socioeconomic status, race and ethnicity, gender, age group, and other factors.

For example, a child who experiences the loss of a parent at a young age is likely to have a dramatically different view of legacy depending on how close his or her relationship was with the deceased parent. The child may understand the concept of legacy more expansively if there was time to spend with a dying parent after a terminal diagnosis, rather than if the parent died suddenly and unexpectedly.

Consider how a parent's perspective on legacy might shift after the death of his or her child from a long illness? Those who have experienced this intense pain may be more likely to spend the rest of their lives inspired to extend and build on the legacy they believe was created by their child during a too-short life.

I was moved recently when I attended a funeral for a twenty-three-year-old family member who was born with many physical and brain ailments. Born to a family with two grade-school boys, Christopher was the third and final child. Even as news of his birth moved through the extended family, it was already clear his life would be filled with struggle.

Since Christopher couldn't speak or care for himself in any way, his parents and brothers adjusted to taking care of his every need. His parents had the difficult task of balancing the needs of their two older boys who'd been born healthy and the needs of Christopher, who required substantial ongoing care. With their extended family members mostly living out of the area, the community rallied around Christopher and his committed parents and siblings. As time went on, their lives continued to incorporate the caretaking of Christopher, even to the detriment of their personal health.

But through the years of caring for Christopher, the family and their supportive community grew close. The impact of this environment was evident at the funeral for Christopher when his two older brothers, now in their late twenties, gave the most incredible eulogies I've seen. Christopher's legacy—forging bonds of love among his community—was fully part of their beings. Even though Christopher may not have been aware he was creating it, his legacy will have strong and long-lasting effects. The outpouring of emotion and sharing wasn't only a defining feature of Christopher's funeral, that energy continues on in the lives of many. I will never forget the experience. It has altered me permanently and I know I'll be sharing the story for years to come. Since values drive so many of our decisions and behaviors, it's critical to make sure our values are communicated as clearly as possible to those we love.

Due to differences in cultural values, parents can leave a legacy of education, caring for family, or philanthropy. For example, individuals of Asian descent often deeply incorporate education into their family structures. In fact, some Asian children are sent to the United States to be educated, and are therefore less connected to their parents for long periods of time. These parents are reinforcing how much they value education and that attitude becomes etched into their legacies.

Families of differing socioeconomic circumstances will communicate legacy differently as well. For example, a child growing up in a blue-collar environment may take away a legacy of hard work, simplicity, and caring about what matters. Many first-generation wealth creators come from blue-collar backgrounds. Often, even though they've created substantial wealth, they never forgot the values of hard work and perseverance they absorbed from their parents. When it comes to the next generation, those first-generation wealth creators could, with intent and care, establish a legacy of helping others.

Many wealth creators guard against creating a legacy of inaction and laziness by promoting and practicing philanthropy with their children. By engaging in philanthropic endeavors, they reduce the potential that their fortunate circumstances will foster entitlement and materialism in their children. In fact, our practice is encountering this active approach among more and more families of various net-worth levels for similar reasons. A focus on family legacy enhances not only the way parents commit to crafting their legacies, but also how children begin to develop a lifelong understanding of the concept.

In a number of important ways, our children are our legacy. Like most parents, you may have asked yourself these difficult questions:

- Am I fostering a sense of entitlement in my child or an awareness of individual responsibility?

- Does my child know that I believe in everything she does, but that I also expect her to pursue her personal potential?

- Is my household a place in which I model positive leadership and where mutual respect is fostered?

Even if we find ourselves falling short of the ideal answers to these questions, we can keep working to get better.

A Legacy of Education

Today, for the most part, a college degree is the functional minimum for young people to enter a career. The bachelor's degree of fifteen years ago may no longer be enough. The current cost of college is substantial and reports from many sources illustrate that U.S. college loan levels are becoming an appreciable problem. Many kids are graduating with college degrees accompanied by large student loans and heading into career paths that don't pay enough to make the math work.

But what about the many college students whose parents pay for college out of savings, college plans, or cash flow? Families of relatively substantial means can cover tuition and associated costs without resorting to student loans. As parents, we want our children to be educated, but should we expect them to participate in the cost of it? Legacy has an interesting resonance in this conversation. The question becomes, whose legacy is the focus? I've witnessed parents who seem to engage in an ego contest to see who can send their children to the most expensive schools without their kids having much, if any, participation in the cost. What is the potential danger?

Parents of this current generation may look back and realize that their kids didn't have enough "skin the game" of their own educational process. We may find that as young adults, they struggle with career challenges and life issues because they've been conditioned to expect things to come easily. Some young people entering the workforce today believe that if they work for a few years, they'll adopt the same lifestyle as their parents. Is this realistic? Of course not, but if we aren't careful, the current generation of parents may be responsible for a legacy of unrealistic expectations that will do their adult children no favors. Struggle is a part of success that we all need to experience for ourselves.

I recently witnessed a family of six grieve the death of the father in his mid-fifties and then with the mother's understandable struggle to cope in the aftermath. In fact, due to these dynamics, the youngest daughter was essentially left without parents as a junior in high school. As she navigated this tremendously difficult time, she had the support of her many high school friends and her siblings. I can't help but think that because this girl has been forced to become an adult overnight, she will likely work through the challenges of life better than most. While she never should have encountered such awful circumstances, it's possible that the coping skills and perspectives she gathers from them will help her become successful. Her legacy may be her perseverance despite the odds and helping others do the same.

Legacy of Ideals or Things

Most people who are asked whether legacy is more about ideals or more about things and accomplishments choose the more altruistic answer: ideals. And legacy is all about our ideals and values—what we find to be most important in life.

In their book *Halftime: Moving from Success to Significance*, when Bob P. Bufford and Jim Collins ask "what is in your box?" they're inviting each of us to examine what's most central value in our lives. But what we say is "in our box" could differ from what actually defines our legacy, now and forever. If we aren't vigilant, we may find that material possessions, pursuits, accomplishments, or fame and fortune, become our legacies. Without an awareness of our purpose and thoughtful intentionality, we could find that our legacies emerge in profoundly different ways than we'd intended.

The bottom line is that we each exert the primary influence over our own legacy—which is challenging and empowering at the same time.

KEY TAKE-AWAYS

♦ Your background and heritage affect how you understand the concept of legacy.

♦ Legacy can be understood, in part, by learning about others' life experiences and observing patterns in the lives of the people around you.

ACTIONS

♦ Define how the legacies of others have influenced your life. Take time to examine—in writing—how legacy impacts your key relationships.

♦ If you have a child, ponder how what you give your child today impacts his or her ongoing view of reality and expectations.

2

An Important Conversation

So why is it so important to cultivate a legacy conversation? Because lives are changed when people focus on what their legacy means. Our thinking tends to shift away from a fixation on immediate happiness and momentary fun toward more thoughtful consideration about the lasting effects of our actions on others.

An awareness of personal legacy encourages the intentional expression of values, beliefs, experiences, aspirations, and relationships. As a result, great things happen, often with a ripple effect that reaches a large number of people. When you care about your legacy, you become the metaphorical pebble in the pond, whose impact spreads far beyond its original scope of influence.

Preparing to become that pebble, though, requires a proactive approach to both everyday choices and overarching decisions. The challenge is that the busyness of everyday life can hinder our ability to recognize and act on legacy-building opportunities. We can easily miss chances to offer a compliment to someone that lifts them up and makes their day. Or we might overlook an opportunity to pay the bill of someone less fortunate at a restaurant or drive-thru. Perhaps we wouldn't watch for a moment to make an impact by leaving a server a thirty percent tip at the diner rather than fifteen percent. How often could a few extra dollars mean a lot to someone who has served us, when we wouldn't miss the same few dollars if they fell out of our wallets?

Helping others doesn't require wealth; it demands awareness. If you slow down and take time to be aware of what's happening around you, you'll find times when you live your legacy by helping someone else.

It's All About Relationships

In his book, *The Seven Levels of Intimacy*, Matthew Kelly describes the ultimate relationship with another in terms of helping someone become a better version of herself or himself. His perspective offers a powerful shift in the way we view the people in our lives, and illuminates the nurturing role we can have in their lives. One result of considering your legacy can be about making sure you frame all your relationships in this positive way. It is just one step, but a significant one.

A few years ago, a retired gentleman behaved in a way that illustrates how to create legacy today through relationships and behaviors with others. The man and his wife retired to Florida. When they first relocated, they lived in a motor home as they waited for their house to be built. Near where they'd set up their motor home, in an underprivileged neighborhood where he appeared quite out of place, he discovered a barbershop that he started to frequent. The business was in an area that was quite a distance, both literally and figuratively, from the fancy new golf-course development where his new house was being built. After the house was done, the man continued to drive more than thirty minutes each way to get his hair cut. Are you wondering why? Turns out the reason he kept returning is that the young guy who owned the place had just bought the business and was working hard trying to support his wife and young children. At the same time, he was running a boxing center—trying to make a difference in the community by keeping kids off the street and away from drugs and gangs. This retired gentleman was inspired by the young barber. He decided that not only was he going to continue to patronize the barbershop, but he would also donate to the boxing center.

It's just one example of someone stepping outside a personal comfort zone to shore up someone else's legacy-building efforts.

Intention or Direction?

Have you ever wanted to do something but it didn't work out the way you intended? If we're being honest, we'll all admit to having that experience, probably more than once. When we attempt to accomplish something, even with great intentions, there's always a chance it will turn out poorly. As the saying goes, the road to hell is paved with good intentions.

On a daily basis, we are treated to political and business leaders talking about how they *meant* to make a difference or *intended* to create change. Their results usually aren't consistent with their goals. As a result, it's easy to start feeling cynical about the very idea of lofty intentions. But without setting ambitious goals, individuals and organizations couldn't implement programs, initiatives, and changes that improve our world.

Fortunately, there are resources available that can help to provide some clarity on this issue. Andy Stanley, in his book *The Principle of the Path*, writes in chapter two: "Direction— not intention—determines our destination."

Where we end up, our destination, is determined by the direction we actually move toward, not the destination we intend to reach. For example, a man who lives in Tampa, Florida, and intends to arrive in Naples, Florida, by heading north on Interstate 75 won't reach his intended destination. Regardless of his level of commitment, he won't reach Naples because he's simply heading in the wrong direction.

Remember that no matter how many people around you are moving in a common direction, it isn't a reliable indication of whether or not they're going where you intend to go. If you're not reaching your destination, you probably need better navigation, not better intentions. So ignore the herd, turn around, and reassess your path. Legacy is much the same way: Your legacy will be determined by the direction you actually move, not the direction you planned to go.

Consider the story of a woman in her seventies who founded a nonprofit organization that worked to protect children from abuse. Her only daughter recognized that her mother was working on something positive and important, but because their relationship was strained, she didn't engage in it with her mother. Eventually, the woman died, leaving the responsibility of leading the nonprofit to her daughter. While she intended that the organization would continue—as the core of her legacy—she failed to communicate her vision to her daughter, making the management transition problematic. What could have been an opportunity to carry on her mother's legacy; was instead an experience of anger and disbelief. The story ended happily, nonetheless, because the daughter decided to take up the mission of the organization and fulfill what her mother started. It's just unfortunate that they missed an opportunity to share the experience with each other.

Legacy is a highly misunderstood concept, especially in light of generational differences. According to a May 2014 study by Paul Schervish and John Havens at the Center on Wealth and Philanthropy, $59 trillion is expected to pass to successive generations from wealth holders between 2007 and 2061. The sheer scope of that transition means it's imperative that a broader message of legacy is communicated across this generational gap. Upcoming generations need to prepare themselves to assume the wealth they'll soon be charged with managing. The amount of good that could come from judicious and humane use of those resources is immense, but if younger generations aren't prepared, our society could experience tremendous untapped potential and lost resources. When I consider these stakes, I'm reminded of Edmund Burke's words, "The only thing necessary for the triumph of evil is that good men should do nothing." Let's not do nothing.

KEY TAKE-AWAY

♦ Remember that it is the direction we're actually heading that determines where we will end up in life, not our intentions.

ACTION

♦ Make a list of the ways your intentions align with or are inconsistent with your current path. As part of this exercise, particularly consider your health and your personal relationships.

3

Common Legacy Misconceptions

As a way to move closer to discovering what legacy means, let's start with what it isn't. Here are a few misconceptions.

Misconception #1: Legacy is just estate planning.

Legacy discussions usually lead to the topic of estate planning. Wills, trusts, and other legal documents that record and direct the implementation of someone's wishes naturally come to mind when discussing legacy. That makes sense, because if we die without addressing these formal arrangements, we leave a legacy of confusion, frustration, and irritation to those we leave behind.

In his book, *Values-Based Estate Planning*, financial advisor Scott C. Fithian calls the typical estate-planning process a trap of "eternal planning." The process typically results in a somber discussion, especially when topics including death, loss of control, and change must be addressed. The entire discussion can be perceived as something negative, which invites procrastination (at least for many among us).

Statistics show that many Americans don't have a proper estate or financial plan. According to the NAEPC Education Foundation, "It is estimated that 120,000,000 Americans do not have up-to-date estate plans to protect themselves and their families in the event of sickness, accidents, or untimely death" (2011 National Estate Planning Awareness Week news release).

So even though estate planning is a critical process for families, it's all too often a neglected one. By expanding the conversation and reframing it as a larger discussion of personal and family legacy, estate planning can be reimagined in a more positive context—which we at The Family Legacy Center hope will result in a more proactive and holistic approach to estate planning.

Misconception #2: Legacy is mostly about death.

Most of the time, legacy conversations happen after a death when relatives and friends reminisce about the times they shared. Some of the recollections and anecdotes might be rather trivial, even light-hearted, attempts to help comfort those whose grief is sharpest. We've all probably been to a funeral where people gather and recall their deceased relative's favorite beer or best off-color jokes. These conversations can make us laugh, but at some point it's impossible not to reflect: "I hope my life won't be summed up like this. My impact on others must amount to more than that? Doesn't it?"

In order to be an active participant in creating your own legacy, it's important to think of it as a *living legacy*. That will encourage you to think less about what happens after your death and more about your choices while you're alive and well.

26

Then you can begin picturing your legacy and making it tangible.

Misconception #3: Legacy is mostly about money.

Recently I was at college orientation with my oldest daughter. As another college dad and I strolled the campus, we came to the new library, which is quite an amazing structure. Hidden behind the postmodern glass exterior is 150,000 square feet of space. At peak hours, the building is occupied by eight hundred students at a time. As we turned the corner of the building, we encountered the name of the building's headline donor in large forged-steel letters. We remarked that it's quite a legacy to have your name emblazoned on a building like that. But how many people will actually be able to do the same? The truth is, legacy has much less to do with money than this rarified example suggests.

Our society tends to provide a distorted view of legacy, largely thanks to the attention-grabbing examples portrayed by Hollywood and the rich and famous. If we believe what we're shown in pop-culture representations all around us, the pursuit of happiness is everything. From frequent marriages to buying any possession they want, everything revolves around how celebrities are viewed and what makes them feel good, which creates the illusion that life is about having things and practicing instant gratification.

Examples of external expressions of wealth are endless, such as a 2008 *Forbes* article showcasing the first billion-dollar home, a 27-story skyscraper in downtown Mumbai. This and other "look at me" expressions of wealth are all around us. Some people will want to spend a endless dollars on a home — because they have the resources to do so. But you have to wonder why they would. As the expression goes, just because you can do something doesn't mean you should.

Even when a famous person does something charitable and positive for others, it's often a transparent strategy primarily designed to enhance his or her public image. That kind of selfish selflessness doesn't offer a very appealing picture of philanthropy.

Furthermore, the millennial generation, usually defined as those born in the last two decades of the twentieth century, have technology at their fingertips and these "get more" images are pressed into their minds at an alarming rate. The result can be a distorted view of not only what life means, but also what legacy means. Whether our children become wealthy or earn modest incomes, their lives have distinct and valuable meanings, but the messages they absorb through the ever-shifting flow of popular culture don't reinforce this truth.

Despite all of the attention-grabbing impediments they face, though, the millennial generation tends to be more focused than their parents' generation on the things in life that matter most, and less focused on material things.

Misconception #4: My legacy can't be influenced today.

Life is filled with difficulties and, let's face it, sometimes we're in the wrong place at the wrong time. It can be tempting to slip into complacency, to fall into believing that things "just happen" to us.

For example, when it comes to health and fitness, we might conclude that our health is purely a result of environment and heredity, factors that aren't in our control. Maybe we just accept that taking multiple medications is mandatory and there's nothing to be done about it. But is that a useful, or even practical, conclusion?

We are surrounded by images of physical perfection from the internet, television, and magazines. The destructive concept of instant gratification is especially emphasized when it comes to physical appearance. The fear of getting fat leads some teenagers to feel inadequate; and because they don't have extensive life context at that age, it can lead to serious consequences. Our children need the adults in their lives— family members, teachers, and other leaders—to focus on what legacy really means and teach them by example.

The weight problem among young people today is a challenge that needs to be met head on. According to the Centers for Disease Control and Prevention (cdc.gov), 12.5

29

million U.S. children, or seventeen percent, are considered obese. Obesity in this study is defined as having a body mass index (BMI) in the ninety-fifth percentile among children of the same age and gender. As a country, we are creating a legacy of obesity that will lead to chronic disease and skyrocketing medical costs later in life.

Upcoming publications from The Family Legacy Center will explore the importance of good health as a factor of legacy further, but essentially our health is something most of us have substantial influence over. The solution to this societal challenge starts with individuals who understand the connection between legacy and good health. Your habits, the food you choose to serve at home, and your fitness routine model your healthy (or unhealthy) values for your children. Our individual daily choices have the potential to accrue into a societal shift that supports our collective health—what a legacy that would be for our children to emulate.

A large part of legacy is influencing, even inspiring, others. When I think back to all the people who have had a substantial influence over my life, I recognize that they were all people I trusted and respected. They were people with whom I'd built a solid relationship over time with a foundation of strong, clear communication.

But it's also possible to be powerfully influenced by someone you've never met. I had that experience recently when I learned the courageous life story of Carole Swoboda.

I heard about Carole a year ago when I got to know some of her family members through our daughters' gymnastics events.

Carole was initially diagnosed with cancer in August 2010 at the age of forty-six. Following her diagnosis, she went through the typical series of treatments and was declared to be in remission. But after a routine body scan in December 2011, Carole and her family were told the cancer was back. The doctors believed the recurrence was likely not completely curable, but thought treatments would suppress it for a significant period of time. For the next nine months, her scans looked good. Then, in August 2012, the cancer was back again in earnest. Carole decided to take a different treatment approach, a macrobiotic nutrition plan. It worked well for a while. In fact, her health and quality of life on the diet was good for more than a year. In January 2014, however, another scan showed the cancer was back and this time the doctors gave her the terminal diagnosis her friends and family were dreading.

I can only imagine the range of emotions Carole and her family were feeling after that news: from sadness and fear to making peace with the inevitable outcome. Anyone in a similar situation has a choice to make, a critical decision about how to respond. Carole decided to demonstrate the true strength of her faith, creating a powerful legacy by sharing her story publicly. In April 2014 she created a video in cooperation with her church that you can view (vimeo.com/92523691). The video is how I "met" Carole and her words have a huge impact on my understanding of what true legacy means.

I'm sorry I never had a chance to meet Carole in person. I'm convinced that knowing her would have been a blessing. It's an honor to share her story and point others to her video so she can continue to spread the message of faith, hope, and love.

Misconception #5: Being proactive about personal legacy is self-centered.

The concept of personal legacy can seem, on its surface, a self-centered thought process. Sometimes even planning our own funeral, making sure all the arrangements are just the way we want them, can be perceived as self-absorbed. After all, the funeral is for our family and friends. So why do we want to put our energy into the effort? Because human beings like to control things, even beyond our own lives. But most people who plan their own funeral are doing it as an expression of love for others. It can save our survivors from a series of emotionally charged and difficult decisions as they grieve.

When it comes down to it, legacy really isn't about focusing on ourselves. Good legacies are the result of a life well lived; they're not about personal gratification.

To redirect a legacy conversation away from the potential pitfalls of ego we only need to ask ourselves: Why are we here? What is our purpose?

A number of years ago, Dr. Hugh Moorhead, a professor at Northwestern Illinois University, asked 250 of the best-known philosophers, scientists, intellectuals in the world a similar question: "What is the meaning of life?" Some offered a guess, while others admitted they had no idea. A number of the distinguished survey participants even asked Moorhead to write them back once he discovered the answer.

If a group of the world's foremost thinkers had limited answers, it's likely that most of the rest of us don't know either. Some people look to God to find meaning in their lives, and they find comfort in faith's journey of discovery. Those who don't have a faith-based worldview may look inward to answer to this question. Regardless of worldview, though, the meaning of our lives is really not about us individually. It is about others. We find true meaning in things only when we put the focus on something other than ourselves.

People for generations have sought to satisfy this need for meaning by seeking personal satisfaction in amassing material things or by focusing on personal happiness. But these activities are pointless because they provide only temporary satisfaction and will never lead to a long-lasting sense of purpose. Most people who have substantial impacts on others will never make the headlines or even be publically acknowledged.

A friend shared with me recently that she encountered such a person when she was seven years old. As a child, she had a love of horses and she met a woman, then in her fifties, at the horse farm they both frequented. This middle-aged woman shared my friend's childhood passion for horses, an interest that wasn't shared by the other members of her family. They spent many hours at the barn riding and taking care of the animals together. My friend learned how to care for the horses and, during the process, learned how to care for others. The lasting impact of this woman's legacy was highlighted almost forty years later when my friend came across someone in her hometown who had spent time at the farm during those same years. They talked about the amazing legacy this woman has and what she meant to both of them. Her legacy wasn't carved into a steel plaque and mounted on a public building—but that doesn't make her legacy any less palpable for my friend and the other young rider, two people whose lives were forever influenced by the lessons they learned from a caring middle-aged woman who mentored them.

Becoming thoughtful and intentional about your legacy forces you to put less energy into seeking immediate happiness and personal satisfaction and more energy into pondering your potential impact on others—and then on taking steps to implement it.

KEY TAKE-AWAYS

♦ It's vital to move beyond the misconceptions of legacy.

♦ Thinking about your own legacy is not a selfish act, it's an exercise in thinking about how you can positively influence others.

ACTIONS

♦ Talk to a friend about your life's purpose and ask your friend about his or her life purpose.

♦ Consider your gifts and interests. How you can you leverage your passions and skills to impact others?

♦ Start a conversation about legacy with a parent or other family member. Be alert for shared legacy goals. Work together to begin defining your family legacy.

4

Living Legacy

Legacy as a concept is largely misunderstood. An online dictionary's first two definitions of *legacy* are: 1) a gift of property, especially personal property, as money, by will; a bequest; 2) anything handed down from the past, as from an ancestor or predecessor.[1]

As the definition illustrates, legacy connects us with the past; it's something handed down through the generations. While my colleagues and I embrace this generational concept for many reasons, the discussion of legacy shouldn't end there. Through discussing the common misconceptions of legacy, we discover that there is an important opportunity to bring the legacy conversation forward out of the pages by focusing on and being present today.

There is hardly a college campus or health care system that has been unaffected by someone's desire to leave a legacy. Buildings named after someone and scholarships in the name of a person that has died are commonplace. For wealthy families, these posthumous bequests are commonly used as part of a complex estate-planning strategy, sometimes to take advantage of healthy tax benefits. While these bequests are important for society in general, let's consider how legacy becomes established for those who don't have vast financial assets? Or what about a family with a relatively substantial net worth who wants to make an impact on their own family and has a narrow charitable focus? This takes some focused

[1] http://dictionary.reference.com/browse/legacy?s=t; accessed July 23, 2014.

discussion from the standpoint of understanding what legacy means in terms of life, not death.

A number of years ago, two women, Michelle and Aleta, retired from their careers as professional bowlers and started a coaching program and pro shop for bowling enthusiasts. Along the way, they decided they wanted to have a focused impact on animal-rescue organizations, a cause they care deeply about. We have all seen the pictures of animals that have been mistreated by their owners, or simply abandoned. Most people are disturbed by these images and can't understand why another human being would treat a defenseless dog or cat in such a cruel way—but Michelle and Aleta decided to do something about it by leveraging their business and their careers. Bowl 4 Animal Rescue (bowl4animalrescue.org) is now a well-attended annual bowling function that has raised a relatively substantial amount of money for local animal organizations that couldn't have raised that much money on their own. Their legacy has extended beyond having impact on the bowling industry and it will be exciting to see how their influence continues to expand.

Barriers to Living Legacy

So why doesn't this kind of strategic legacy building come naturally? Why don't most people share these retired athletes' approach? One good reason is that we all struggle with a few things that keep us from taking an active approach to our own legacy. These barriers to a living legacy are essentially mindset roadblocks that become barriers to our own potential.

When we're kids, anything is possible. Talk to any ten-year-old and they'll paint an exciting and very detailed picture of their future. Their world is filled with possibilities firmly rooted in a positive attitude. Unfortunately, life has a way of extinguishing the energy that lights our ideal path. As we age, we become more "realistic" and we tend to frame our future in terms of past failures and negative experiences. We all know people who've fallen into that trap; hopefully you won't look in the mirror someday and come to the realization that you've joined them. Short-term thinking, selfishness, a negative attitude, and a victim mentality block us from taking the living-legacy approach to life. We must be on guard against a mindset that keeps us from living fully because when we do, we ultimately rob the world of the benefit of our own potential. Leadership expert and author John C. Maxwell puts it well: "The greatest day in your life and mine is when we take total responsibility for our attitudes. That's the day we truly grow up."

Source of a Mindset

I am fortunate to not only spend time around entrepreneurs,

but to have operated as one for the last twenty years. And I do view it as fortunate even though having an entrepreneurial mindset is one of the most difficult, risky, and disruptive directions one can take. I appreciate what a values-driven, ethical entrepreneur does for the world economy and the human spirit. To be clear, I'm not talking about money-focused, purely greed-driven business people—their values don't match the kind legacy we're advocating. It's the entrepreneurs who embody the spirit of true leadership who bring positive change. It's the same kind of attitude that drives immigrants to overcome great struggles on the way to success.

So when it comes to the subject of living legacy, I can think of no better viewpoint to embody than that of an entrepreneur. While studying what contributes to entrepreneurial success, I've learned that entrepreneurs share a common mindset, regardless of their field of endeavor.

- They have a willingness to take full responsibility for results. They expect nothing.

- They believe that in order to receive value *from* the world, they must first provide value *to* the world—in that order.

- They never give up on their passions. They won't accept that something is impossible.

40

- If they don't see something in the world that represents their vision, they create it.

- They view the world and their circumstances with a sense of gratitude. This applies whether things are going well or poorly.

This entrepreneurial mindset is a critical foundation for those who want to shape a living legacy. The good news is that being an actual entrepreneur isn't required, but adopting some of their characteristic mindset will encourage breakthroughs in your legacy process.

Whether we realize it or not, everyday people exemplify this mindset though they may be unaware they're living out entrepreneurial principles. For example, what about the parent who pays attention to their own health and leads their family in the same direction? In our instant-gratification society, with processed food everywhere and schedules so packed that there's no time to exercise, we could say that it is nearly impossible to be healthy. Regardless of these apparently insurmountable circumstances, they make it happen and lead their family to the same result. Living legacy is about leadership, whether it is the leadership of one or many.

A living legacy means that instead of just making plans for what happens with our money and possessions after death, we develop a plan for living out our values and ideals now. This two-fold strategy ties together life and death into an active and immediate approach to legacy.

Getting Help from Others

One of the fascinating things about being human is that even though we desire to find our own way in life and determine our direction, we eventually come to the realization that we need others. As we strategize and live out our own legacy, help from others is essential.

First, it's difficult to see clearly what we need to change about ourselves. Legacy is about being honest about our shortcomings and how we need to change. The Bible tells us that while we can easily see the splinter in another's eye, we can't see the log in our own. As we share life's journey with others, we must remember that those close to us can see us in ways we can't on our own. Having the willingness and humility to accept their guidance will enhance our own legacy in many ways.

Second, it's easy to assume our successes are the results of a series of our own good decisions. But in reality, individual success depends on the blessings of good relationships. When I reflect back, I realize that a few key relationships have had lasting impacts that helped set me on my current path. Can't we all say the same?

KEY TAKE-AWAYS

♦ Approaching your legacy as a *living* legacy requires you to be proactive and take on the proper mindset.

♦ As a way to prepare yourself to live your legacy, it's useful to study the entrepreneurial thought process.

ACTIONS

♦ What relationships are you most grateful for? Why? Have you told those people how much you value them?

♦ Ask your mentor what one or two things are holding you back the most? Ask him or her how you might overcome those obstacles and move forward on your legacy path.

5

Practical Applications of Legacy

Legacy seems like a fairly simple idea. In the developed world, people typically live their lives by developing relationships, having families, getting educated, and eventually impacting others through a career or vocation. They will be remembered for what type of person they were and what they did.

For all of us, a legacy conversation involves steps that The Family Legacy Center describes as Your Legacy Voice, a continuum, of which is described in the following illustration and description.

Who You Are—your values, experiences, education, family background, culture

What You Give Back—charitable donations, mentoring, community involvement

What You Have—money, possessions

A truly exceptional legacy comes out of understanding where you come from and clarifying your values. That is, essentially, *Who You Are*. This part of legacy planning makes me think of the words of Michael Reddy, part of the Strategic Coach® Program, "If you get stuck and need to make a decision, reconnect with your values, and the answer will be there."

In our wealth management practice, my colleagues and I ask clients a simple question: "When it comes to family, if you could put more emphasis on passing along your values or your money, which one would be the focus?" In other words, if you had to choose between the two, which would you choose? It comes as no surprise when their answer is values. But how many people are intentionally and actively putting their energies into passing along their values? How many wealth holders would actually leave their heirs with no money if they believed they didn't share common values? Not many. We have come to realize that often money is the engine of legacy, but the values are the vehicle that the engine powers to head in a certain direction. And it's the direction that matters most.

Charitable giving is a commonly discussed topic not only among professionals in the advisory services businesses, but also among churches and not-for-profit organizations. There are different views on this topic, from the concept of tithing in the church to trusts paying to a charity at death. But charity is only part of the *What You Give Back* section of Your Legacy Voice. This conversation should also touch on mentoring and community service.

Recently a man told me that his focus with his family was to influence his grandchildren's values. He believes it is increasingly difficult for young people to understand the importance of values thanks to the negative influences of contemporary culture. This form of giving back, we could argue, is just as important as leaving money to a particular organization. For good organizations to thrive in the future, good people are required, which demands an investment of resources by those who understand values. So whether we focus on influencing family or non-family, our next generations need us to broaden our collective understanding of giving back.

Finally, your legacy voice completes with addressing money and possessions, referred to as *What You Have*. The financial services profession and most of the public believe legacy is mostly about money and those who leave a legacy are the ultra-wealthy. But regardless of wealth, legacy is important to all of us.

When it comes to managing wealth, addressing all of the money aspects of our lives is critical. But in addition to money, another aspect of *What You Have* refers to possessions, those things that are handed down through families—for example, family photos, silverware, or furniture. Planning to manage these plays a significant role in living a legacy today. Rather than waiting until after death occurs for the family to sort out the items, consider having an intergenerational discussion today. These types of conversations often result in productive and fulfilling exchanges.

A fifty-year-old gentleman recently told me about his experience of deciding what to do with with family possessions after a long time period. One of the items was antique wood from a barn that had been torn down decades earlier. He was unclear about what should happen to the wood. Because nobody in his family expressed an interest in the wood, he stored it in his garage for years. Finally, since he has a knack for woodworking, he decided to start making some furniture out of the eighty-year-old lumber. His decision to take action transformed something unwanted into breathtaking heirloom works of art that will clearly be part of the family legacy going forward.

A proactive approach to legacy that focuses first on values can be a tough concept to grasp. The thought process is vague and conceptual and not typically the most comfortable discussion. In our world of scientific discovery, there's almost always a formula for solving a problem or understanding how something works. Admittedly, math is not the first thing that comes to mind when discussing the concept of legacy because the concept itself is so nebulous. But most of us seem to share a hard-wired desire to understand things in a practical way.

In developing a formula for the concept of understanding our own legacy, there were a number of factors to consider. First, life serves up a constant stream of circumstances that we can't control. Events happen every day and we have to individually decide how to handle them. So essentially the only control we have is over our personal response to these events.

Stephen R. Covey makes this point in his book, *The 8th Habit*. "Between stimulus and response there is a space. In that space lies our freedom and power to choose our response. In those choices lie our growth and our happiness." There is a great deal of personal control in this "space" between stimulus and response and surely we've all wished for a do-over, or as it's called in golf, a mulligan. Maybe it was an overreaction or perhaps a disappointing lack of reaction to something that required a response.

If there were a formula for our own legacy, what would its individual components be? Considering that we face many things we do not control, how can the factors be represented in an equation that will allow us to be proactive in our quest to realize a meaningful legacy?

Your Legacy Quotient SM TM

$$LQ = (V + E) \times P \times R$$

The formula says: *Your Legacy Quotient* equals your *Values* plus your *Experiences* leveraged by your *Passion* and your *Resources*. Here is an abbreviated breakdown of the formula's components:

V = Values

Defining personal values is the starting point and foundation of the process because your values mark the compass that defines your own individual true north. The Family Legacy Center's research demonstrates that focus of this stage in the process is to brainstorm about what is most important by narrowing down your core values, those nonnegotiable principles that you hold to be true under all circumstances. Not unlike an organization that has to define its purpose for existing, individuals must also define what we hold most important. What ideals direct our choices and will we never surrender?

Categories of Values

1. Spiritual values: faith in God, fellowship, good works

2. Emotional values: compassion, kindness

3. Educational values: academic achievement, life-long learning

4. Work values: efficiency, hard work, success

5. Recreational values: sports, travel, hobbies

6. Cultural values: visual art, theater, music, dance

7. Economic values: financial responsibility, frugality

8. Personal values: loyalty, independence, fairness

9. Ethical values: responsibility, honesty, integrity

10. Philanthropic values: financial generosity, volunteering

11. Physical values: health, wellness, exercise

12. Public values: citizenship, community involvement

13. Material values: possessions, social status

14. Relational values: family, friends, colleagues

The world has a way of influencing the direction our lives will lead. Cultural influences are a powerful force that push and pull us through a lifelong battle. These are the reasons our values are so important.

A sailboat with no rudder will be forever pushed in whatever direction the wind desires. Only when we decide to put the rudder in the water will we regain control over the direction of the vessel. Our values serve the same purpose as the rudder, steering us where we should go as the wind of life tries to influence our direction. Only when we have confidence in our own values can we be clear about what direction we are heading.

E = Experiences

Next, the formula says to add experiences together with core values. The experiential factor includes educational background, personal life experiences, and key lessons taught by others. These experiences are what give core values practical application in everyday life, transforming the abstract notion of values from something conceptual to tangible. Once your values are clearly defined and combined with practical experiences, then we can start to leverage them for maximum impact.

P = Passion

Passion is the fuel that powers the engine of knowledge toward high performance. It is part of the leverage section of **Your Legacy Quotient** SM TM. Passion is any powerful or compelling emotion or feeling—love or hate. For our purposes, the key part of the definition is *powerful.*

The power of passion drives a worthwhile effort through difficulties that might otherwise stop your forward momentum. Joe Torre, former manager of the New York Yankees, once referred to the ability to get up after getting knocked down as one of the keys to having success. It's heartfelt passion that provides the determination to get back up when the logical mind says no. Passion, as part of the sailboat metaphor, is like the sail, when opened wide, it results in lasting momentum.

R = Resources

Finally, legacy is leveraged by another factor, resources. This component is fairly broad, including relationships, money, and possessions. Defining resources broadly—beyond monetary values—emphasizes that one can have an incredible legacy that has absolutely nothing to do with money. This is a refreshing corrective that helps redefine the common message of pop culture.

Relationships are considered resources because they are something of value that must be developed and maintained. Like money, they can be lost and they're nearly impossible to recover if not treated with high value.

KEY TAKE-AWAYS

♦ Your legacy voice is a discussion tool that can help us recognize that our legacy emerges out of who we are, what we have, and what we give back.

♦ We can proactively work on our legacy by remembering **Your Legacy Quotient** SM TM: $[LQ = (V + E) \times P \times R]$ Your legacy is a combination of your values and experiences multiplied (leveraged) by your passions and resources.

ACTION

♦ Prioritize your values and share them with someone close to you. Discuss the elements of your Legacy Quotient and that of your friend or family member.

6

Continuing the Conversation

The Family Legacy Center's hope is that legacy becomes an important conversation in your life. It is the one thing we all have in common, regardless of race, age, economic status, gender, or ethnicity. Feeling the call to contribute to something bigger is what gives us the desire to live, to learn, and to thrive. Some call it hope. Some call it vision. We wrap it all together and call it legacy.

Going forward, we will explore other important legacy topics. Health and fitness, for example, have been mentioned several times in this book. In my conversations with various physicians, they've all agreed that the key to good health is about something much bigger than just changing some habits. For all of us, changing habits is very difficult, especially when it comes to fitness. When we finally get the motivation to go to the gym and exercise, the next challenge is figuring out how to get started. We may ask ourselves: Should I sign up for a class? Should I kickbox? How do these crazy machines work?

Then, if we break through our inertia and actually get started, we have to maintain our momentum to be successful. Experts say we need to stick with something for at least twenty-one days to create a new habit. So if our current habit is no exercise, then the new habit of exercise has to last for at least three weeks. Then, even if we do create the new habit, often something compels us to take a break from the exercise, albeit temporarily. And, you guessed it, we take a break for twenty-one days and suddenly we've reestablished our habit of no exercise. How do we break free from the cycle? Maybe the secret is to tie your health into something much bigger and beyond you: your legacy. We have to understand healthy choices in more expansive terms or we won't make them part of who we are. Good health needs to be about who we are, not just something we participate in.

Despite the fact that my business means I spend most of my time around baby boomers and elders, I truly enjoy the millennial generation. This group, born after 1980, is the technology generation, the "need it now" generation, the "just Google it" generation. But they're also a generation of individuals who think deeply when given the opportunity. They care about things beyond money and possessions and doing something that matters is a priority. Life is something to be enjoyed and work is part of a work-life balance. They tend to want to be part of a team, rather than charge ahead by themselves as a pioneer. Of course these are generalizations, but this group is distinctive. Many of them have watched their parents go through divorce. Many of them have watched their parents chase money and possessions as the end goal rather than a byproduct of pursuing a vision. Future Family Legacy Center publications will explore how millennials view the concept of legacy and what they intend to do about it. We are committed to helping them understand it fully and, by extension, have a big impact on the world.

Until next time!

Epilogue

Our hope is that you begin the important legacy conversations as a result of reading this book. Why?

Because regret is something we have all experienced at one time or another in our lives. Sometimes when we take action in a particular situation we regret the way we handled it. Other times, we ignore something and after we can no longer affect an outcome, we feel a sense of regret.

A good friend of mine frequently says **"Prevention is measured in ounces and regret is measured in tons"**.

Our hope is that you can use some of the ideas presented here to have conversations with those you care about to avoid regret in your life. We hope to inspire conversations that focus on prevention.

.

About the Author

Christopher (Chris) Cousins is an advisor with the firm Financial Architects, Inc., in Farmington Hills, Michigan. He holds two designations from the American College of Financial Services: ChFC® (Chartered Financial Consultant, 2002) and RICP® (Retirement Income Certified Professional, 2014), and is continuing his education in philanthropy and generational wealth.

Since joining Financial Architects in 2004, Chris has been committed to working with clients in the retirement stage of life. Legacy is a very real concept for his clients, so in 2013 Chris cofounded The Family Legacy Center, an organization focused on fostering and expanding conversations about our living legacies.

Ten years ago, Chris had his initial experience with writing and publishing when he participated in the nationally known book, *Masters of Success.* The book held the top position on the Wall Street Journal Best Seller list in June 11, 2004.

Chris and his wife Susie have two daughters, Ella and Olivia. Among other interests, he enjoys playing drums in a band whenever they get the chance to play.

Reader's Notes

_____

_____

_____

_____

_____

_____

_____

_____

_____

_____

_____

_____

_____

Made in the USA
Charleston, SC
18 September 2014